Exploring th...

Meg Cichon García

Contents

Rigby

A Harcourt Achieve Imprint

www.Rigby.com
1-800-531-5015

Looking for Adventure

Imagine that you're sailing away to places far from your home. You're ready to explore lands you've never seen before. What do you think you'll see on your trip? What type of people will you meet?

Hundreds of years ago, many people decided to travel so that they could explore the world. Let's learn about some of these very curious people.

In those days, **explorers** from Europe were sailing to the Americas for the first time. Even though Native Americans had lived here for many centuries, Europeans had never seen this land before. When they visited this place, they discovered many opportunities.

People lived in the Americas long before European explorers arrived.

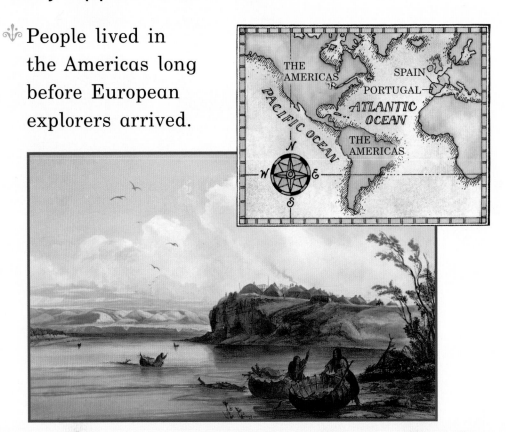

Ever since then, people have been exploring the Americas. Some people have searched for riches. Others have tried to learn more about these great lands and the people who have lived here for so long.

⚜ Some explorers wanted to learn about new lands.

Juan Ponce de León

Juan Ponce de León was a Spanish explorer who traveled to the Americas from Spain. He wanted to search for gold. He settled first on the island of Hispaniola. Then he moved to Borinquén, an island that we now call Puerto Rico. The Taíno people lived there.

⚜ Ponce de León came to the Americas to look for gold.

6

Ponce de León and his crew took control of the island. They turned the Taínos into slaves. Ponce de León forced the Taínos to look for gold, and most of the Taíno people died searching for it.

❧ Ponce de León met Native Americans in the lands he explored.

The Fountain of Youth

Back in Spain, the king was growing old. He had heard tales about a Fountain of Youth whose special waters could make people young again. The king wanted Ponce de León to find this unusual fountain.

⚜ King Ferdinand and Queen Isabella encouraged explorers to discover new lands for Spain.

So Ponce de León left Borinquén in search of the fountain. He soon spotted land, but there was no Fountain of Youth. Instead, Ponce de León found an area covered with beautiful flowers. He claimed this **territory** for Spain, and because he arrived there around the time of Easter, he named it *Pascua Florida.* This means *Easter of Flowers* in Spanish. Today that land is part of the state of Florida.

❧ Ponce de León
and his companions
searched for the
Fountain of Youth.

Meeting the Calusa

Next Ponce de León and his crew sailed down the eastern coast of Florida, around the tip, and up the western coast. Along the western shore, they met the Calusa people. The Calusa were known by many people for their strength and force. The Calusa refused to give their land to these unfamiliar people. Ponce de León and his men soon returned to Borinquén.

⚜ The Calusa tribe lived in Florida before Ponce de León arrived.

A few years later, Ponce de León came back to Florida with 200 settlers, determined to establish a Spanish **colony.** But the Calusa were prepared to fight for their land. Ponce de León had to return to Borinquén once again.

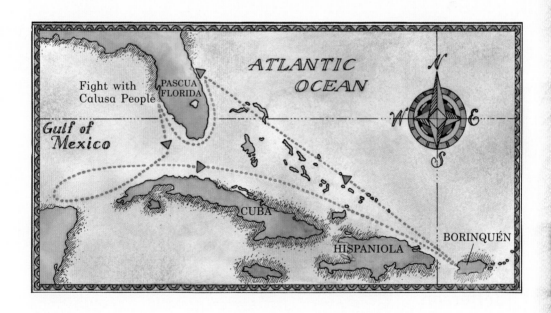

Lewis and Clark

Nearly 300 years after Ponce de León arrived in Florida, people were still curious about North America. What did it all look like? Who lived there? And how big was it? When Thomas Jefferson became president of the United States, he decided to answer these questions.

Thomas
Jefferson

A Special Journey

President Jefferson asked Meriwether Lewis to go on a special journey. Jefferson wanted Lewis to explore the western lands of the United States and make maps of the territory. Lewis invited his friend William Clark to join him.

Meriwether Lewis

William Clark

About 50 men joined Lewis and Clark. One year later, they set sail on the Missouri River. Soon the group reached what is now Omaha, Nebraska. There they met the Oto and Missouri peoples. Lewis and Clark presented them with peace medals, American flags, and gifts. They promised the Native Americans a peaceful future.

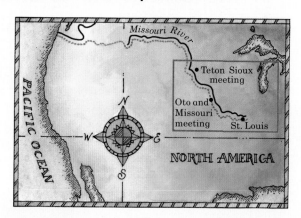

Fun Fact

Traveling along the Missouri River was very slow. These explorers were pleased if they traveled 14 miles a day!

The explorers continued their journey to what is now Pierre, South Dakota. The Teton Sioux people lived and traded there. The Sioux believed that Lewis and Clark wanted to control their territory. The two groups grew upset with each other, and a battle nearly started. Black Buffalo, the Teton Sioux chief, stopped the argument by ordering his soldiers to stop fighting.

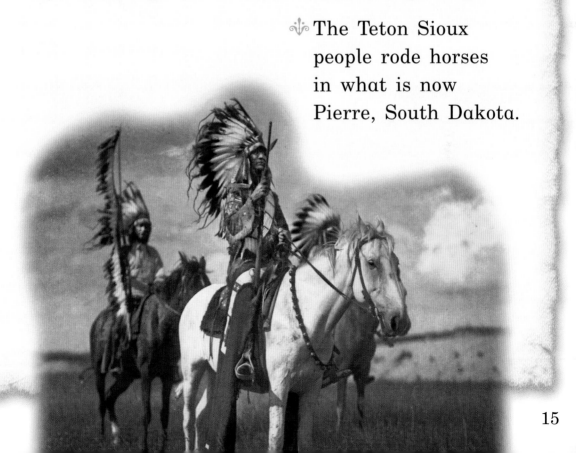

⚜ The Teton Sioux people rode horses in what is now Pierre, South Dakota.

The explorers stayed with the Teton Sioux for a few days. The Teton Sioux gave them buffalo meat as a peace offering.

Lewis and Clark might have turned the meat into buffalo jerky, or dried meat. Because it was easy to make and easy to carry, it was a popular meal for travelers.

Recipe for Buffalo Jerky
- buffalo meat
- salt and pepper

1. Cut the meat in long strips.
2. Sprinkle the meat with salt and pepper.
3. Put the meat on sticks and lay over the campfire to dry overnight.

Unexpected Friendships

Lewis and Clark soon left South Dakota to continue their journey on the Missouri River. When winter came, the group settled in a Native American village near what is now Bismarck, North Dakota. Lewis and Clark needed to talk to the Native Americans in order to learn from them, but the explorers were unable to speak the Native Americans' language.

Lewis and Clark
met Sacagawea,
a Native American
woman who helped
them. Sacagawea and
her husband could
speak to both the
Lewis and Clark
group and the Native
Americans. So Lewis
and Clark invited
Sacagawea and her
husband to join
them. Together they
traveled to what
is now Montana.

⚜ Sacagawea was
a Native American
woman who helped
Lewis and Clark.

The group then traveled through the Rocky Mountains. They were very tired and hungry when they reached what is now the state of Idaho. They arrived in the land of the friendly Nez Percé people.

⚜ Lewis and Clark traveled through the Rocky Mountains.

The Nez Percé taught Lewis and Clark how to make new canoes from pine trees. The explorers could now complete their journey on the Columbia River. The explorers traveled on to what is now the area of Washington and Oregon, the western edge of North America.

❧ Lewis and Clark traveled by canoe along the Columbia River.

There's More to Explore

Ponce de León and Lewis and Clark explored for different reasons, but they had one thing in common. They wanted to see the world and all that it had to offer.

Even though most of the lands on our Earth have already been explored, there are still large areas, such as oceans and outer space, that curious people want to explore.

☙ This is Explorer I, the first U.S. spacecraft.

Glossary

colony a new place where people live but are still ruled by their original country
explorers people who travel to places they have never been to before
territory land or area

Index